Poetry Of Christmas

By Leigh

ISBN: 978-0-9794612-3-1

Dedication:

I dedicate this book to the One whose birthday it honors, Jesus Christ.

Many say the 'Jesus is the Reason for the Season' and rightly so. But it is also true that He thought the 'Reason for the Season' was the souls of men, and came to earth wrapped in a human body to die in order that we may one day live forever in His presence, giving Him praise, honor, wisdom, thanks, and glory forever and a day!

Thank you Lord for coming to earth to die for us!

I would also like to honor my Illustrator, Jim Tracy. While he is still in high school, he has a God given talent that he is even now honing just like artists much older than his 16 years. He practices it daily and gives God glory and thanksgiving for this blessing he has received. Thank you, Jim for taking time to bless this book with your unique gift!

The Road To Bethlehem

Illustrated By: Jim Tracy

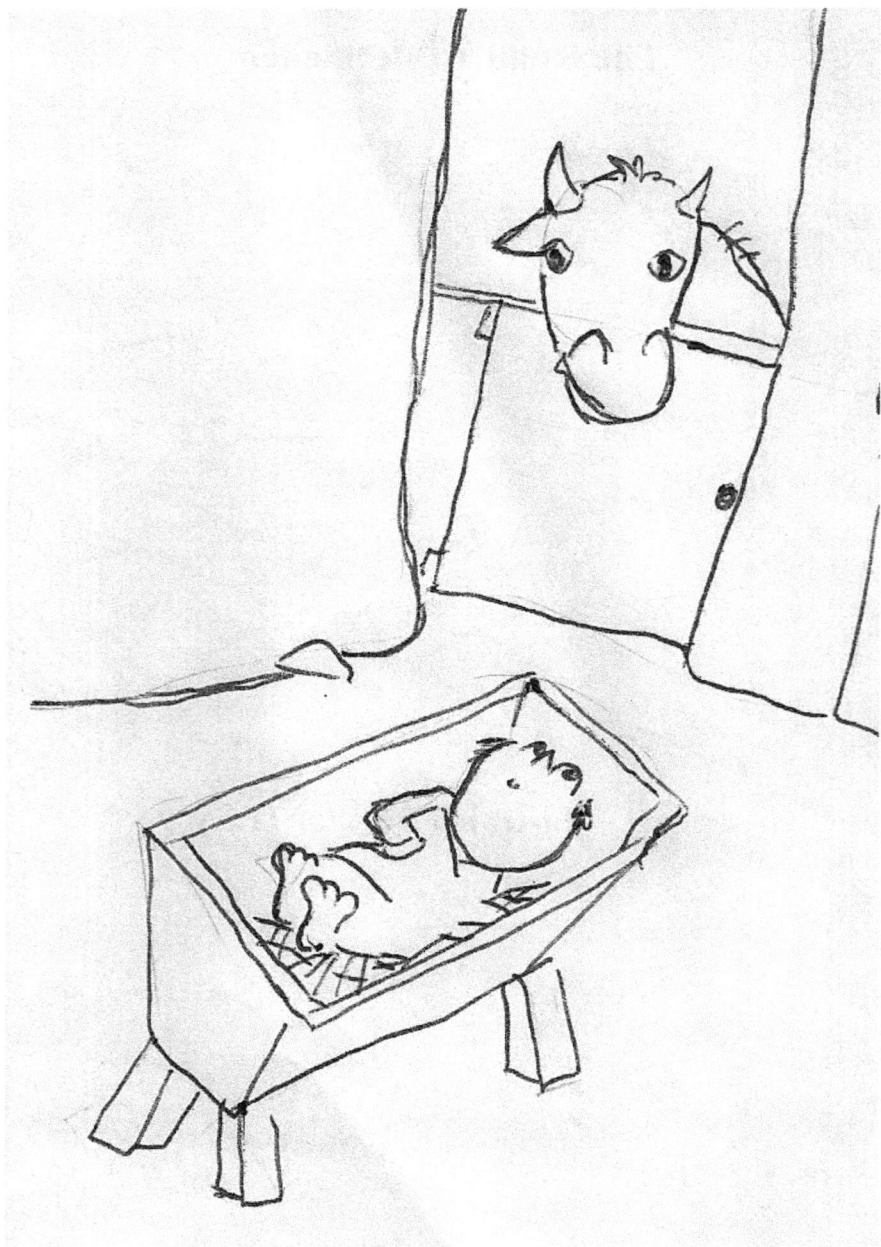

Mary And Joseph

We took the road to Bethlehem
My beloved and me
For Cesar had a census called
A new tax had decreed

From Galilee the road was harsh
We walked along the way
Traveling in a caravan
To keep the thieves at bay

In Bethlehem the crowds grew thick
The inns turned us away
There was no place to make a bed
Save a manger in the hay

My love was soon to bear a Son
A Child of Holy birth
The one of whom Isaiah told
Would one day come to earth

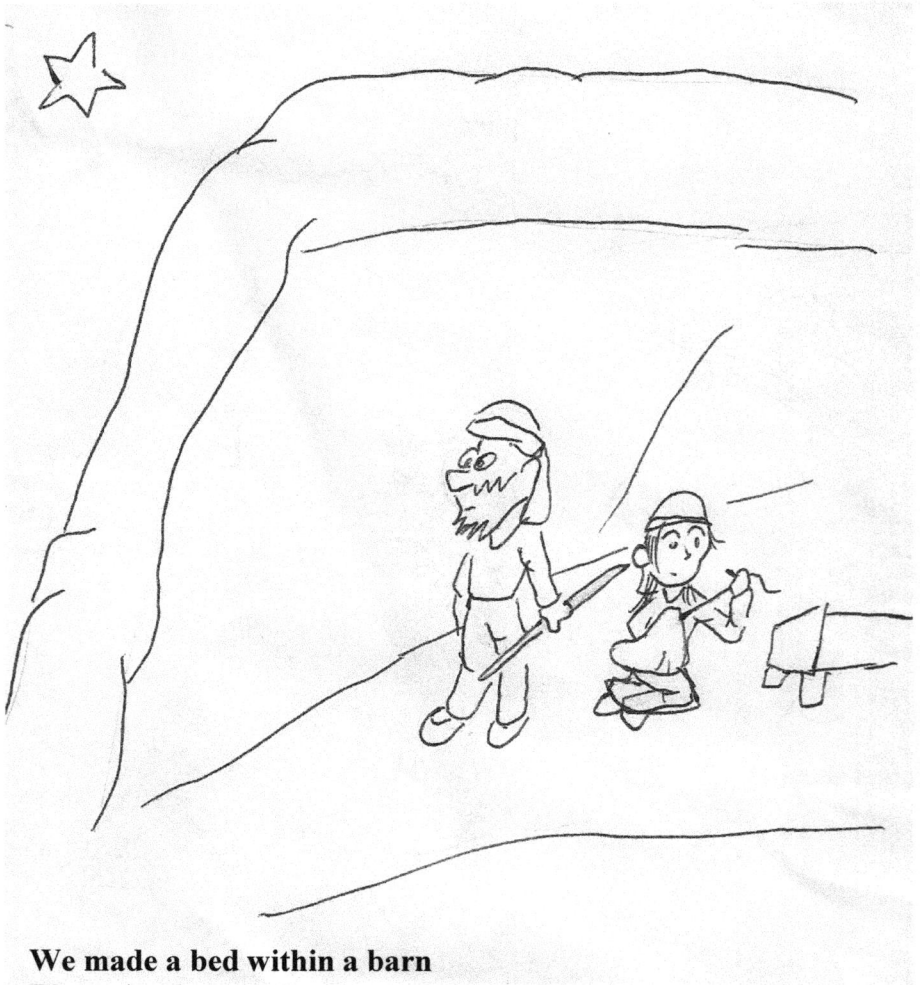

We made a bed within a barn
The animals gave us room
A bed of hay, sweet and clean
A bright starry sky to drive away the gloom

The Shepherds

The road to Bethlehem we took
Late one starry night
The angels came and sang a song
God's glory gave them light

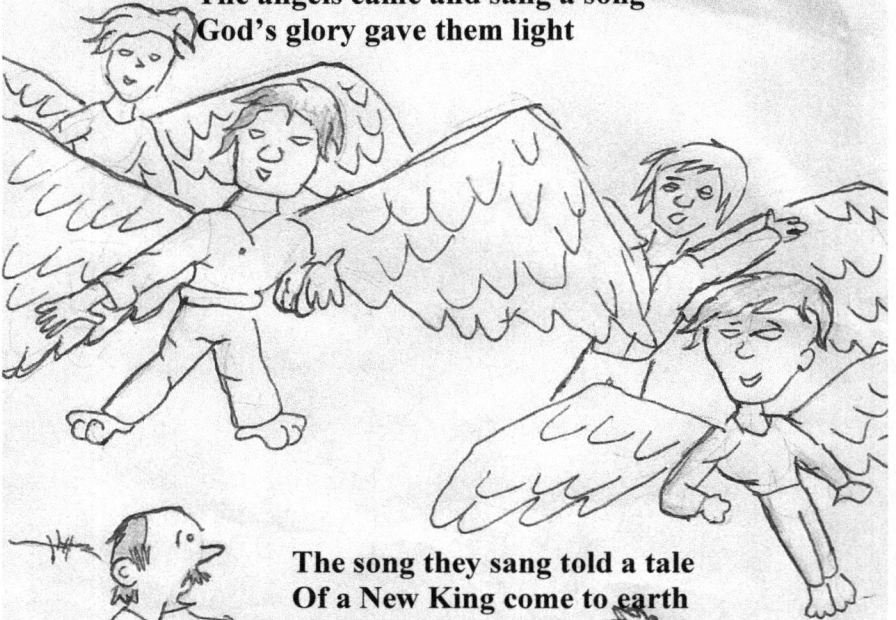

The song they sang told a tale
Of a New King come to earth
A Baby born in Bethlehem
And of His lowly birth

They sent us down to tell the crowds
Of the Savior God did send
We left the sheep there on the hill
To take the road to Bethlehem

The Angels

The angels' song led to a cave
Where ox and donkey lay

The manger where they ate their food
Was where our New King played

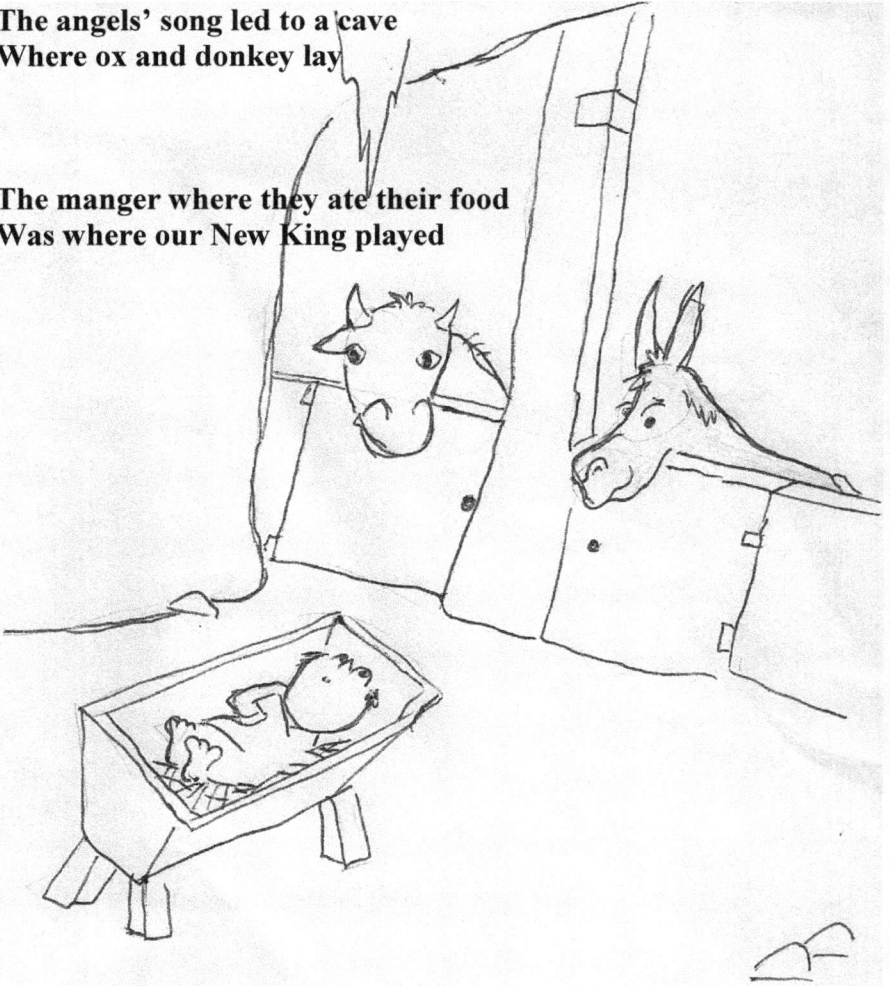

When we found the resting place
Of the Savior come to earth
Our hearts were filled with love and peace
Our souls were filled with mirth

We shared the news of Jesus' birth
With those who filled the street
We told them of the King of kings
Who slept among the sheep

We took the road from Bethlehem
Back up the darkened hills
To join the sheep and get some sleep
Our hearts with joy He fills!

The Wisemen

We took the road to Bethlehem
To follow a shining star
The prophets told in stories old
Of a King to be born a far

The journey on the road to Bethlehem
Was fraught with toilsome days
We traveled by night
To see the star's light
'Twas our guide all along the way

A caravan of traveling kings
From the East we came
To greet the King whose star we'd seen
And to shed abroad His fame

To the Holy City of peace we came
Of the new King to inquire
But the magistrate became irate
When we told of this new Sire

King Herod

The court astrologers came to tell
Of the Messiah long foretold
And of the star that would guide the way
With a light for all to behold

They told the king that Bethlehem
Was the place where this Child would lay
The king relayed this news to us
And sent us on our way

But in the night while following the light
The Lord did warn our hearts
And told us to go and visit the Child
But in another direction to depart

The star did stop above a home
Upon a Bethlehem street

We followed it right up to the door
The new King we came to greet

The mother did invite us in
The father standing guard
We took our gifts inside the house
Our camels filled the yard

Within the home we opened our chests
Our presents to present
Bags of gold, jars of myrrh
And vials of frankincense

Precious gifts of greatest worth
To honor the King of kings
God's only Son has come to earth
Salvation to us He brings

We took the road from Bethlehem
Across the continent
The angel's warning se did heed
And another direction we went

Mary, Joseph And Jesus

We took the road from Bethlehem
To Egypt we did flee
My beautiful bride, the Child fair
The king's gifts, and me

Egypt Land

We lived among strangers there
The Child's life to save
When God sent His angel to bring us home
I fear I was not brave

The king who sought to kill the child
Had passed away, and yet
His family was still upon the throne
Which caused my heart to fret

Home To Nazareth

We turned aside to Galilee
To Nazareth town we moved
Back to the place where we began
The home that we had loved

The Roman World

The Roman world does believe
That all roads lead to Rome
And yet we find through these tales here
This is not true for some

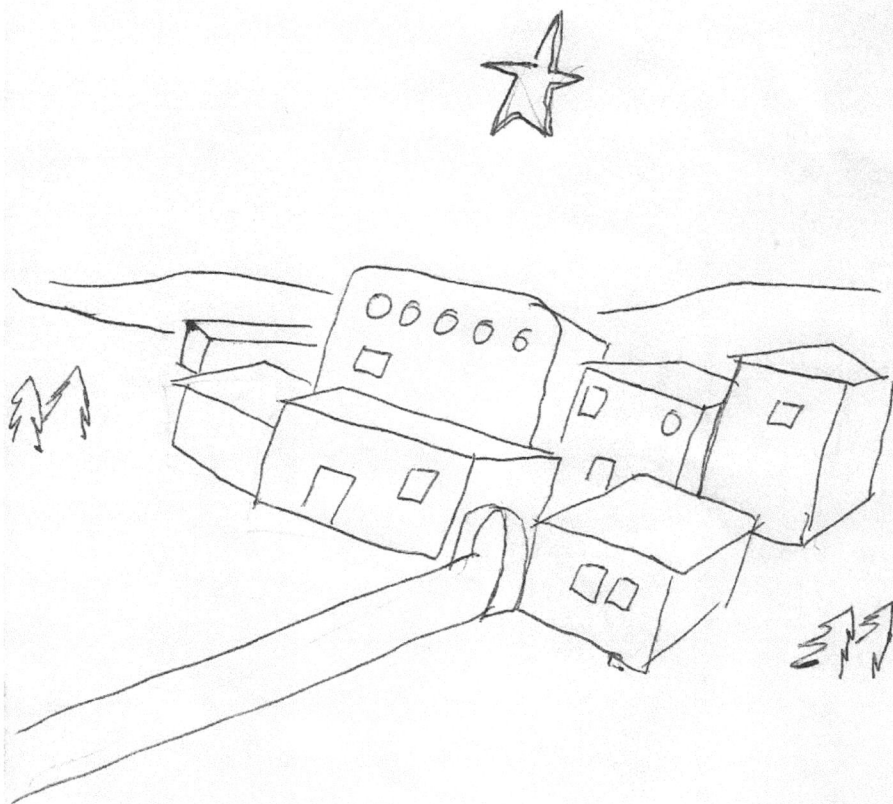

These travelers to Bethlehem
Have forever changed the earth
For each has played an important part
In the story of Salvation's birth

Christmas Angels

As the angels sang
Christ was born
That very first
Christmas Morn
Let us join with them
And sing their song
And invite others
To sing along!

~*~

"And there was with the angel a multitude of
heavenly host praising God, and saying;
Glory to God in the highest, and on earth
peace, good will toward men." Luke 2:13, 14

What Is Christmas?

Christmas is more than just Santa and such
Santa is nice, but He isn't enough
Christmas is more than just Holly and wreaths
These may be pretty, but are so incomplete
Christmas is more than just wrappings and strings
Pretty as they are, they are still only things
Christmas is more than the presents we give
Presents are great, but they won't help us live

Christmas is for Jesus' birthday you see
He came down to earth just to die on a tree
He loves us all that his life he did give
He laid it down so that forever we'd live
Trust in Him and just call on His name
He'll save you from sin; He has taken your blame

So what is the reason for Christmas, you ask
It is the day God decide to start winning us back
He sent us His Son as a babe on the hay
Jesus came on that very first Christmas Day
Jesus was born in the town of Bethlehem
The shepherds were told and the wisemen knew when
He was born in a stable, in a manger he did lay
The Inns were all full, their keepers sent them away

Christmas is for Jesus' birthday you see
He came down to earth just to die on a tree
He loves us all that his life he did give
He laid it down so that forever we'd live
Trust in Him and just call on His name
He'll save you from sin; He has taken your blame

Angels came singing to announce Jesus birth
They told of the reason He came down to earth
They told the shepherds and then flew away
The shepherds' cam to visit the very same day
The wisemen came from the east very far
The had learned of a new King and followed His star

But no one else in the earth seemed to hear
The birth of their Savior seemed to fall on deaf ears

Christmas is for Jesus' birthday you see
He came down to earth just to die on a tree
He loves us all that his life he did give
He laid it down so that forever we'd live
Trust in Him and just call on His name
He'll save you from sin; He has taken your blame

The wisemen stopped in city of peace
But the king was not happy to see them in the least
His councilors told him of the star in the sky
He spoke to the wise men, he was being so sly
He asked the travelers again to return
He wanted the home of this new King to learn
But he was only trying to save his own neck
Soldiers killed the baby boys and their homes did wreck

Christmas is for Jesus' birthday you see
He came down to earth just to die on a tree
He loves us all that his life he did give
He laid it down so that forever we'd live
Trust in Him and just call on His name
He'll save you from sin; He has taken your blame

Even as a babe men were seeking His life
Joseph hid Jesus and Mary, his wife
To Egypt they traveled and lived for a while
They lived on the gifts the wisemen gave to the Child
Joseph was told in a dream one dark night
The king was now dead, they could return from their flight
Joseph was scared, did he dare return home?
He'd heard the king's son had taken the throne

Christmas is for Jesus' birthday you see
He came down to earth just to die on a tree
He loves us all that his life he did give
He laid it down so that forever we'd live
Trust in Him and just call on His name

He'll save you from sin; He has taken your blame

The family did to the town Nazareth move
Mary and Joseph returned to the place they had loved
Jesus grew up in stature and grace
He knew that one day he would be taking our place
His cousin John did prepare the way
And Jesus was baptized by him one great day
Ministering for three years all over the earth
He was telling all men that they needed new birth

Christmas is for Jesus' birthday you see
He came down to earth just to die on a tree
He loves us all that his life he did give
He laid it down so that forever we'd live
Trust in Him and just call on His name
He'll save you from sin; He has taken your blame

Jesus did the rile up the Religiously Right
So they gathered the soldiers and took Him by night
In the darkness His disciples had fled
To a kangaroo court our precious Savior was led
They questioned Him, beat Him and spat in His face
They pulled out His beard; it was such a disgrace
They sent Him to Pilate who sentenced Him to die
Then lead Him to Calvary there to crucify

Christmas is for Jesus' birthday you see
He came down to earth just to die on a tree
He loves us all that his life he did give
He laid it down so that forever we'd live
Trust in Him and just call on His name
He'll save you from sin; He has taken your blame

They buried our King in a borrowed tomb
And for nights three days such a heaviness did loom
But the third day the earth shook, the stone rolled away
The disciples saw Jesus and there was rejoicing that day
He told them to tarry for the Spirit to fall
Then to travel the earth sharing His message to all

When He had done all He was sent to complete
He returned to heaven and took up His seat

Christmas is for Jesus' birthday you see
He came down to earth just to die on a tree
He loves us all that his life he did give
He laid it down so that forever we'd live
Trust in Him and just call on His name
He'll save you from sin; He has taken your blame

He's coming back soon, His bride to retrieve
Are you one of us? He wants no one to leave
The marriage supper we'll attend with our King
There will be feasting and dancing and praises to sing
Hallelujahs will chorus thru the heavenly halls
Forever their echoes will bounce off the walls
For this is the reason that Christmas was given
God wanted all peoples with Him to be forever livin'

Christmas is for Jesus' birthday you see
He came down to earth just to die on a tree
He loves us all that his life he did give
He laid it down so that forever we'd live
Trust in Him and just call on His name
He'll save you from sin; He has taken your blame

Thank You, Jesus for coming on Christmas to give
Salvation to all so that with you we would live!

Christmas is for Jesus' birthday you see
He came down to earth just to die on a tree
He loves us all that his life he did give
He laid it down so that forever we'd live
Trust in Him and just call on His name
He'll save you from sin; He has taken your blame

Son of Man ~ Son of God

Born of Mary, born of God
Through the earth, like us, He trod
Battled Satan like we do
To prove He was a man like me and you

Prayed the Father, "Not My will"
Before He walked up Calvary's hill
There He paid for all our sin
Victory over death to win

He showed us how this earth to trod
This Son of Man ~ This Son of God!
~*~
Thank You, Jesus!
Happy Birthday!

~*~

"But He held His peace, and answered
nothing. Again the high priest asked
Him, and said unto Him, 'Art thou the
Christ, the son of the Blessed?' And
Jesus I am, and ye shall see the Son of
man sitting on the right hand of power,
and coming in the clouds of heaven."
Mark 14:61,62

Getting Ready for Christmas

Christmas Candy, sticky and sweet
This is what the children would eat
But Mom's in the kitchen
The ham in the oven
What a wonderful way she has
Of showing us her lovin'

Dad's in the back yard
Shortening the tree
So it fit in the front room
For all to see

Grandma's baking cookies
Papa's in the shed
Packing out the stockings
White and green and red

Auntie's in the parlor
Stringing popcorn for the tree
Her chain would be getting longer
If it wasn't for me

We're all getting ready for Christmas
Whatever it may take
The Pies are on the buffet
But where's the birthday cake?

You know it's Jesus' birthday
A celebration for our King
What gift will you bring Him?
What songs will you sing?

I baked a cake for Jesus
The best I ever made
I put flowers on the borders
And chocolate in the glaze

A made a gift for Jesus

And put it in a box
I wrapped it with red paper
But the ribbon was full of knots
Inside my gift was simple
A heart of paper gold
I wrote a verse upon it's back
And here my story told

I give my heart to Jesus
My Savior and my king
And though it's made of paper
It is my dearest thing

I do not have much money
To buy a costly gift
But Lord, this paper heart
Is worth more that all of it

A picture of all that's in my mind
To give to You, my King
For if I could, I would
Give You my every thing!

The feast is on the table
The candle's burning low
The family has all gathered
On each face is a glow

We're ready to celebrate Christmas
The Birthday of our King
We give thanks for all we have
And to Him our praises sing

Happy birthday Jesus
I'll save you a piece of cake
Thank You for the Love You brought
And that all my sin You take!

Happy Birthday Jesus
My Savior and My King

Praises I will raise to You
And I'll give You everything!

The Gifts We Bring

Merry Christmas to you
Is what we always hear
But do you know whose birthday
Comes this time of year?

It's the birthday of our Savior
Born to be the king
Gather 'round Him quickly
Your best gifts do bring

Not of Gold nor Silver
Not of beads and string
Gifts of Praise and Worship
These to Him, we bring

Happy birthday, Jesus
This we gladly sing
Sharing Your gift with loved ones
While we give You everything!

www.ingramcontent.com/pod-product-compliance
Lightning Source LLC
Chambersburg PA
CBHW030306030426
42337CB00012B/604